Getting Around!

By Felicia Law

Pictures by Barry Rowe

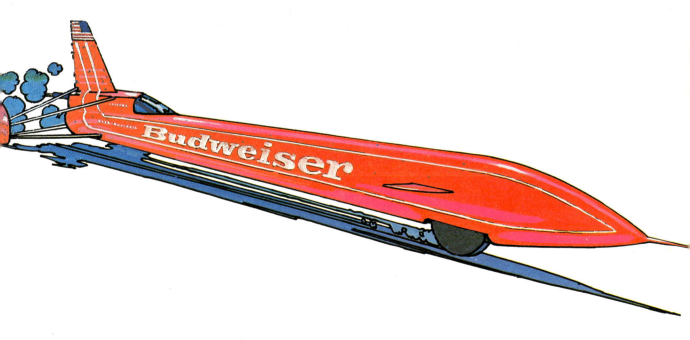

Gareth Stevens Publishing
Milwaukee

BRIGHT IDEA BOOKS:

First Words!
Picture Dictionary!
Opposites!
Sounds!

The Four Seasons!
Pets and Animal Friends!
The Age of Dinosaurs!
Baby Animals!

Doctor Wotsit's Zoo!
My Day at School!
Old Farm, New Farm!
Your Favorite Fairy Tales!

Mouse Count!
Time!
Animal ABC!
Animal 1*2*3!

Homes Then and Now!
Other People, Other Homes!

Dressing Up!
It's Fun to Cook!
Make It with Odds and Ends!

Space Trip!
Getting Around!
On Wheels!

Library of Congress Cataloging-in-Publication Data

Law, Felicia.
    Getting around!

    (Bright idea books)
    Previously published as: Ways we move. 1980.
    Bibliography: p.
    Summary: Offers facts about various means of transportation, from kayak to space shuttle, with related activities.
    1. Transportation—Juvenile literature. (1. Transportation) I. Rowe, Barry, ill. II. Title.
TA1149.L39   1986   629.04   85-30438
ISBN 1-55532-044-9
ISBN 1-55532-019-8 (lib. bdg.)

This North American edition first published in 1986 by

Gareth Stevens, Inc.
7221 West Green Tree Road   Milwaukee, Wisconsin 53223, USA

U.S. edition, this format, copyright © 1986
Supplementary text copyright © 1986 by Gareth Stevens, Inc.
Illustrations copyright © 1980 by Octopus Books Limited

First published in the United Kingdom as *Ways We Move* with an original text copyright by Octopus Books Limited.

Typeset by: Ries Graphics ltd.
Series Editors: MaryLee Knowlton and Mark J. Sachner
Cover Design: Gary Moseley
Reading Consultant: Kathleen A. Brau

Contents

The Kayak

A kayak is like a canoe with a covered deck.

Eskimos used kayaks to hunt seals. They covered the wood frame with animal skins. Today, kayaks are covered with canvas, plastic, or fiberglass.

Most kayaks carry one person. But some can carry two or four people.

Kayaks are used for sport and for racing.

The Submersible

Submersibles are small ships. They travel underwater with a crew of two or three people.

Submersibles are used for underwater exploration. Sometimes they are used to fix other ships or objects that are underwater.

Some submersibles have long arms or pincers. They are used to bring things to the surface.

The Motorcycle

A motorcycle has a gasoline motor and two wheels with rubber tires.

Like a bicycle, the motorcycle is steered with the handlebars.

Most motorcycles have a pedal for the rear brake and a hand lever for the front brakes.

Some motorcycles can go faster than others. Faster motorcycles have larger engines and heavier bodies.

The Fighter

A fighter plane is part of a country's air force.

This plane is a U.S. Air Force F-15 Eagle. It can fly up to 1,650 miles an hour.

The F-15 has very modern equipment to help the pilot find a target.

The Parachute

People use parachutes to jump out of airplanes and float to earth.

A parachute is made of cloth. It is packed into a container. The parachutist wears the container on his or her back.

After the parachutist jumps, he or she pulls a cord. This releases the parachute.

The Hydrofoil

The hydrofoil is a boat. It rides above the waves on metal rods.

These rods are like wings on a plane. When the boat goes fast, they lift it out of the water.

When the hydrofoil slows down, it goes back to the surface of the water.

Hydrofoils can go as fast as 90 miles an hour.

The Hovercraft

The hovercraft is a boat. It rides just above the water.

Strong jets of air are blown under the hovercraft by a large fan. The air shoots out around the boat and lifts it above the water. Other boats must push their way through water.

Hovercrafts can go as fast as 70 miles an hour. They can also go over land.

The Helicopter

A helicopter can fly forward, backward, and to either side. It can land and take off straight up and down. It can fly low and quickly change direction. It can also hover above one spot.

The helicopter is lifted by the main propellers. The small propellers at the tail give it balance.

The Tank

Tanks are heavy military vehicles. They have large tracks over their wheels. These tracks let them move over rough ground, across streams, and up hills.

Most tanks have a turret on top with a large gun. The crew is protected by the tank's thick metal armor.

Roller Skates

A roller skate has four wheels.
Inside the wheels are little metal
balls. They are called bearings.
They make the skate's wheels
turn smoothly.

Good skaters can skate forward
and backward and in circles. Some
people skate in the park. Some
skate in rinks. They may dance,
play hockey, or race on roller
skates.

The Bicycle

A bicycle has two metal wheels covered with rubber tires.

A chain connects the back wheel with the pedals. When the rider turns the pedals, the chain makes the back wheels turn.

Most bicycles have hand brakes. They make rubber blocks press against the wheels. This slows the bicycle down.

The bicycle is steered with the handlebars. It takes time to learn how to balance on a bicycle.

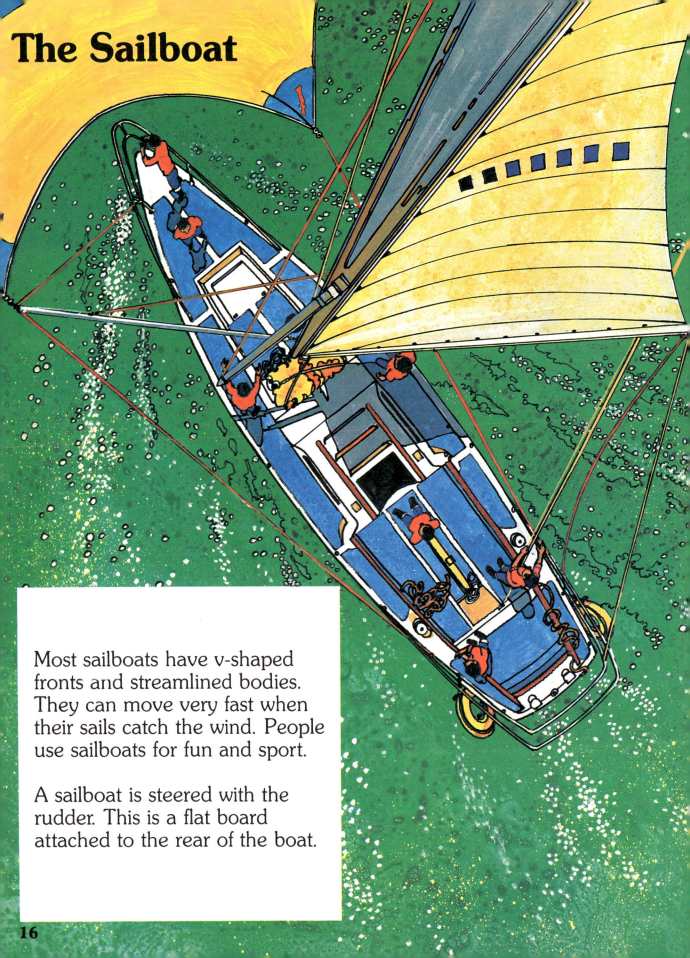

The Sailboat

Most sailboats have v-shaped fronts and streamlined bodies. They can move very fast when their sails catch the wind. People use sailboats for fun and sport.

A sailboat is steered with the rudder. This is a flat board attached to the rear of the boat.

The Balloon

Most balloons are made of strong, thin material, like nylon. They are filled with hot air or a gas like helium.

The balloon floats because it is lighter than the air around it. It will come down when the gas or air inside it is slowly let out — just like a toy balloon!

The Bobsled

Bobsleds carry two or four people.

They are made of wood or metal. They are usually painted in very bright colors.

Bobsleds slide over ice and snow on metal runners. They can go more than 90 miles an hour.

Bobsledders push the sled to start it. They jump in once the sled is moving and steer it with a rope attached to the front runners.

Skis

Skis are long and flat. They are curved upward at the front and are worn with ski boots. They are used to travel down snow-covered mountains and hills. They are also used to travel on snow-covered flatland.

The skier uses two poles to push with and for balance on turns.

The Moon Buggy

The moon buggy runs on a battery and travels over very rough ground.

The buggy carries a video camera and other equipment to explore the moon. American astronauts used the buggy to collect rock and dust samples during some of the Apollo flights in 1971 and 1972.

The Jeep

Jeeps are cars that can travel across rough ground.

They were used as military vehicles in World War II. Now they are also used as pleasure cars.

The jeep shown here is called a Cherokee. Like all jeeps, it has four-wheel drive. This means that the engine turns all four wheels. It also means extra power and control on bumpy or snowy ground. In most cars, the engine only turns two wheels.

The Ocean Liner

An ocean liner is a large passenger ship.

It cannot cross the ocean as fast as an airplane. In fact, it is like a large hotel. Passengers can relax in deck chairs and swim in the pool.

At night, they can eat in the ship's restaurants. Then they can dance and enjoy a show.

VTOL

VTOL means Vertical Take-Off and Landing aircraft.

A VTOL has a special engine. It can take off and land straight up and down in a small space. Once it is in the air, it flies like a regular airplane.

VTOLs are used by air forces all around the world. The VTOL is still too small and too noisy to be used as a passenger plane.

Supersonic Aircraft

Supersonic aircraft can travel faster than the speed of sound. Sound waves travel at a speed of more than 650 miles an hour.

One supersonic plane is called the Concorde. It can travel at more than twice the speed of sound.

When a supersonic plane goes faster than sound, it makes shock waves in the air. These shock waves make a sound like thunder. This noise is called a sonic boom.

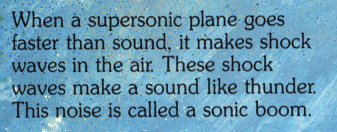

The Excavator

Excavators are large tractors. They have a big bucket on an arm that moves.

The driver digs the teeth of the bucket into the ground. The bucket then scoops up huge loads of earth.

Excavators clear the ground for roads. They also dig holes for new buildings.

The Drag Racer

A drag racer is a special car. It moves very fast in a short race of a quarter of a mile.

The drag racer has a very large engine. It also has large rear wheels with smooth tires. Its front wheels are small and light.

Two cars at a time race in a drag race. They zoom down the drag strip. The winner is the first to reach the quarter-mile line.

Some drag racers can go as fast as 200 miles an hour.

The Cruiser

A cruiser is a warship.

This cruiser hunts submarines.

It carries a helicopter on its deck. It uses its radar and helicopter to search for ships.

Cruisers like this one are much smaller than giant warships such as aircraft carriers.

The Oil Tanker

Oil tankers are ships that carry large amounts of oil.

The largest oil tankers are supertankers. They may be 1,200 feet long. That is as long as four football fields!

The tanker's oil is pumped below the deck.

The tanker's engines, control room, and cabins for the crew are usually at the rear of the tanker.

The Container Truck

Goods are often shipped in large metal containers.

Containers are usually carried on ships. When the ship docks, the containers are unloaded.

Some are lifted onto the back of a truck. Others are loaded on trains.

Containers are one safe way of sending goods.

The Land Speed Record Car

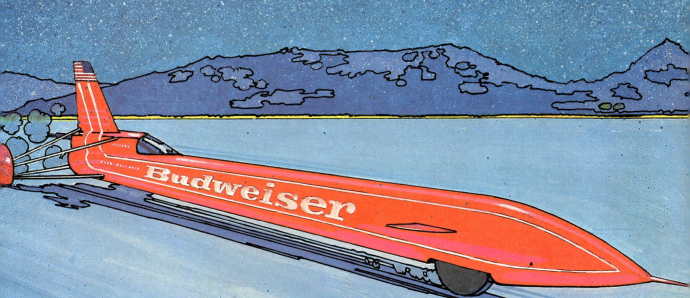

Some cars are built just for setting speed records. They usually have a jet or rocket engine.

In 1979, the Budweiser Rocket car set a new record on the Bonneville Salt Flats. This is a large, flat place in Utah.

The Rocket set a record speed of 638.6 miles an hour.

The Sand Yacht

The sand yacht has three wheels and a sail. It races on sandy beaches.

Its body is long and thin, like a canoe. It is made of fiberglass.

The sail catches the wind. This moves the boat forward. Sand yachts sometimes go four times faster than the speed of the wind.

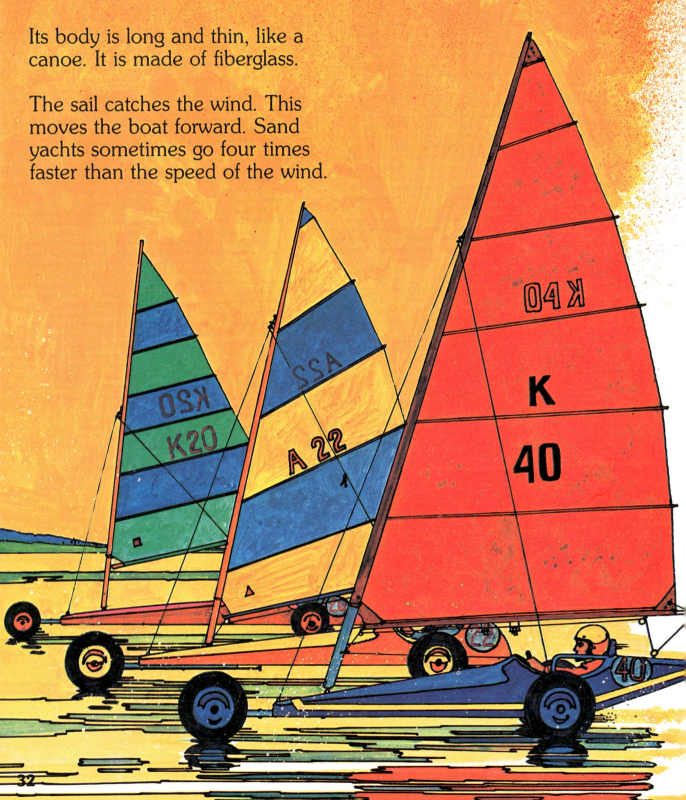

The Windsurfer

Windsurfing combines surfing and sailing.

The windsurfer looks like a large surfboard with a sail. The rider is also called a windsurfer.

The rider steers by moving up and down the board and by turning the sail.

The Subway Train

Subway trains run on electric tracks beneath large cities like New York, London, and Paris.

Passengers reach the subway by going down escalators or stairs.

They ride the subway from one part of the city to another.

The Submarine

The submarine is a ship that can go underwater.

To go underwater, a sub fills its tanks with sea water. It is then heavy enough to sink beneath the waves. To come back up, the sub empties the water. It then has enough air in its tanks to rise.

Some submarines are nuclear-powered. They can stay underwater for a very long time.

Subs can fire rockets and torpedoes underwater.

The Car

The automobile, or car, has four wheels and, usually, a gasoline engine.

There are many different kinds of cars, such as sedans, station wagons, and sports cars. Most are made by very large companies.

People use cars to go between home and work or to take weekend or vacation trips.

The Train

There are many new kinds of trains. They are very fast and very safe.

This Japanese train is called the Bullet Train. Bullet Trains travel to many cities in Japan. They have electric engines and run at 130 miles an hour.

The Bullet Train is driven by an engineer. It also has automatic computer controls. They tell the engineer when to speed up or slow down.

The Racing Car

Racing cars are very fast. They are driven on racetracks. Sometimes the tracks have many steep curves.

This car is a Ferrari. Ferrari racing cars are always bright red. This is the racing color of Italy. Ferraris have won many races all over the world.

The Snowmobile

Snowmobiles have a motor and skis in front. They are driven over deep snow and steered with handlebars.

Some snowmobiles can go as fast as 100 miles an hour and are often used in races. They are also used by police and medical people to help people in snowy places.

The Hang Glider

A hang glider is like a large kite. It has wings and a metal frame.

The flier holds onto a metal bar attached to the frame. The flier steers the glider by moving along the bar.

The flier runs down a steep hill to take off. The air under the wings lifts the glider into the air.

The Space Shuttle

The space shuttle can take off into space and land on earth.

When a rocket or satellite is launched, it can make just one trip.
But a shuttle can make many trips.

The shuttle is launched like a rocket. Its fuel tank drops off as the shuttle climbs into space.

When it is orbiting the earth, the shuttle is a space laboratory. There, astronauts discover new things about life in space.

The following "Things to Talk About and Do," "Fun
Facts About Getting Around," and "More Books About
Getting Around" offer grown-ups suggestions for
further activities and ideas for young readers of
Getting Around!

Things to Talk About and Do

1. What gets you around? Car? Subway? Bus? Talk to someone who gets around another way. What are the differences?

2. Which of the vehicles in Getting Around! would you like to have or use as a place to work? What would you do?

3. Pick one of the recreation vehicles that interests you — for example, the sailboat, the balloon, or the windsurfer. See if you can find more books about them. Or maybe you know of someone who operates one. Tell your friends or family what you find out.

4. Find a place where one of the vehicles in this book operates. Write a short report with a picture of what you observe.

5. Go to your library and look up accounts of the latest space shuttle mission in the newspapers. What was the purpose of the mission? Did anything unexpected happen?

6. There are downhill skis and water skis and cross country skis. How are they different? See if a sporting goods store in your area has all three kinds and check them out. Otherwise, check books at your library or bookstore.

Fun Facts About Getting Around

Here are some of the first, fastest, biggest, longest, and best things about getting around.

1. The longest ship canal is the Suez Canal in Egypt. It is 100.6 miles long and was built in 1869.

2. That same year, 1869, America's coast-to-coast railway opened.

3. The largest submarine is the USS Ohio, 560 feet long.

4. The largest aircraft carrier is the USS Nimitz, 1,088 feet long.

5. The largest passenger liner is the Queen Elizabeth II, 1,000 feet long.

6. In 1804, the first locomotive traveled 10 miles on tracks in Wales.

7. The first American-built locomotive, Tom Thumb, made its debut in 1829.

8. The speed record for a steam train is held by the British Mallard at 126 miles per hour.

9. The longest rail line is 5,800 miles from Moscow to Nakhadka, across Siberia.

10. The longest rail bridge, the Huey P. Long in Metairie, Louisiana, is 4.4 miles long.

11. The world's first underground railway opened in London in 1863.

12. The first fighter tank was the British Mark I, built in 1915.

13. December 17, 1903, is the date of the first successful powered air flight. Orville and Wilbur Wright's Flyer became the first airplane.

14. The first hot air balloon that could carry passengers was built in France in 1783. (And by the way, before airplanes, balloons were used to carry military personnel into the air on observation platforms.)

15. In 1930, Amelia Earhart became the first woman to cross the Atlantic in a solo flight.

16. The fastest rail train is the French TGV, with a top speed of 186 miles per hour.

17. The Boeing 747 is the largest jet. It can hold 47,000 gallons of fuel, enough to fly from Europe to California.

18. An automobile is 80% steel, and its average weight is 2,120 pounds.

More Books About Getting Around

Here are some more books about getting around. Look at the list. If you see any books you would like to read, see if your library or bookstore has them.

Aircraft: A Latimer Factbook. Maynard/Paton (Rand McNally)
Aircraft that Work for Us. Freeman (Children's Press)
Ballooning: High and Wild. Adler (Troll)
Busy Trains. Lippman (Random House)
Challenge! The Big Thunderboats. Stone (Troll)
Encyclopedia of Transport: Air. Storer (Silver Burdett)
Encyclopedia of Transport: Land. Pick (Silver Burdett)
Encyclopedia of Transport: Space. Kerrod (Silver Burdett)
Encyclopedia of Transport: Water. Pick (Silver Burdett)
Future Travel. Abels (Crestwood House)
I Can Read About Motorcycles. Troll editors (Troll)
I Can Read About Racing Cars. Troll editors (Troll)
I Can Read About Trucks and Cars. Troll editors (Troll)
Motorcycles and Mini-Bikes. Troll editors (Troll)
Mouse and the Motorcycle. Cleary (Dell)
Moving a Rocket, a Sub, and London Bridge. Paige (Children's Press)
Paper Airplane Book. Simon (Viking)
Space Flight: A Latimer Factbook. Cowley (Rand McNally)
Tales of Flying. Fearon Pittman editors (Fearon Pittman)
Tales of Railroads. Fearon Pittman editors (Fearon Pittman)
Train Whistles. Sattler (Lothrop, Lee & Shepard)
Trucks You Can Count On. Magee (Dodd, Mead)

For Grown-ups

Getting Around! is a picture book that gives primary grade children a chance to develop their reading skills as they learn more about a subject of great interest — transportation. *Getting Around!* appeals to children's familiarity with such conventional means of getting around as cars and subways. It also appeals to their fascination with space travel, sport vehicles (including roller skates and land speed record cars), and such exotic forms of transportation as the hydrofoil, the hovercraft, and vertical take-off and landing aircraft. In addition to the wealth of basic facts offered in the main text, the "Things to Talk About and Do," "Fun Facts About Getting Around," and "More Books About Getting Around" sections give children further opportunities for reading and learning.

The editors invite interested adults to examine the sampling of reading level estimates below. While reading level estimates help adults decide what reading materials are appropriate for children at certain grade levels, they are nonetheless no more than estimates.

Most reading specialists agree that efforts to encourage young readers should be based not only on reading level estimates but on practice in reading, listening, speaking, and drawing meaning from language. These activities, which encourage young readers to use language beyond the scope of the text, are developed in the supplementary sections of *Getting Around!* These activities also give adults a chance to participate in the learning — and fun — to be found in this book.

Reading level analysis: SPACHE 2.4, FRY 2, FLESCH 91
(very easy), RAYGOR 3, FOG 5, SMOG 3